Believe in Miracles
Lessons from the animals at Last Stop Horse Rescue

Stories told by Joyce Pomeroy
Written by Toni Helen
Illustrations by Deb Lindsay

A gift for

_____

With Love From

Believe in Miracles
a new beginning . . .

True stories of love, trust, friendship, and hope
for children of all ages

Dedication by Joyce Pomeroy

This book is dedicated in memory of my dad, Ken Pomeroy. His unconditional love and support gave me courage to pursue my dreams. Having him in my life was a miracle in itself so "Believe in Miracles" as the title of this book is just as dear to my heart as the message I hope it brings to all who read it.

To my five beautiful grandchildren: Kenny, Kimberly, Connor, Emma and Siena. May you all grow up to be kind, caring, and generous with a strong love for family and God.

To my daughter, Toni: for writing this book so children can share in lessons about *believing in miracles* from the horses at Last Stop Horse Rescue. And thank you, Toni, for also believing in our own personal "miracle"... "Welcome to Georgia, Grandmommy!"

To Deb Lindsay: for her beautiful illustrations bringing these stories to life with her extraordinary- yet modest- talent. More importantly; Thank you, Deb, for your kind heart, unconditional devotion to Last Stop Horse Rescue, and for our friendship. "Love knows no distance..."

To my beloved equine soulmate, a thoroughbred named Rem. You left much too soon; May your spirit run free.

I also want to thank all the volunteers and supporters who share in these miracles with me. I truly could not do this without you!

© Copyright 2015 by Joyce Pomeroy, Last Stop Horse Rescue. All rights reserved.

Cover illustration by Deb Lindsay: "You are safe" shows Joyce with little Gracie and big Belle at Last Stop Horse Rescue.

HOWDY!

My name is Joyce and I live on a big farm. It is a special kind of farm. It is a rescue farm that helps horses! Some horses are sick. And some are hurt. Some even need food and water! Because I love animals so much, I take care of these horses. I help them to feel better!

Horses come to my farm from many different places. Some can be nervous and scared when they arrive. They may even be afraid of people! This may because someone bad tried to hurt them. When something like that happens, it can take a long time for horses to learn to trust people. But that is another way I help them- I teach them to trust by showing how much I love them!

I also help find good homes for horses with families that I know and trust- families who will love them as much as I do!

Do you know that animals can teach us many new things? They may not be able to talk to us using words, but they can talk in their own special way! If you listen to an animal with your eyes instead of your ears you may be able to hear what they are saying. The way an animal moves can say a lot about how they feel.

For example, if a horse is running and playing with other horses, it is probably happy and having fun! But if a horse is angry, it may let you know by pinning its ears back quick and sharp. Sometimes when a horse is nervous or afraid it will stand still holding its breath.

Did you know that horses can sleep standing up? They can and often do! So how do we know the difference between a horse that is nervous or afraid and a horse that is just taking an afternoon nap? Usually if a horse is just sleeping, its eyes are closed and one of its back hoofs may even be bent in a relaxed position.

Also, if a horse is limping or walking funny, it could mean they are hurt or injured and need help from an animal doctor, called a *Veterinarian*.

So as you can see, we can learn a lot about animals by watching them and listening with our eyes. They are able to tell us how they are feeling. I love watching the horses at my farm because they "talk" to me all the time!

And this is how my adventure began . . .

For many years I helped rescue people. I wore a uniform and rode on fire trucks and ambulances! I also worked at a hospital with doctors and nurses taking care of sick people.

As I got older I was not able to work anymore. That made me sad. I missed rescuing people so I decided to rescue a pony instead. Her name is Emma!

EMMA'S STORY: Promise made, promise kept

I have always loved animals, especially horses. Emma is a pony who had seven different homes in 10 years! The reason Emma had so many different homes was because she was not a pony that people could ride. This was not Emma's fault. Emma had never been trained to ride! Nobody ever showed Emma what a saddle even was! They just assumed she already knew.

Poor Emma... people would climb up on her back and kick her to go but this made Emma scared and confused. She did not know what to do so instead she did nothing!

The people thought Emma was misbehaving by not listening to their commands. They got mad at this innocent little pony and decided they did not want her anymore. Emma was given away- home after home, family after family- by people who thought she just was not good enough. This hurt Emma's feelings.

Emma began to think that nobody would ever want her. Until one day, I came along and found her. I wanted Emma! I thought she was perfect! She was perfect for me because I did not want to ride her; I just wanted to love her! And do you know what? She loved me just as much as I loved her! We became best friends!

I learned from Emma that everyone is "perfect" for something- or someone. You just have to find out what that something is. I was perfect for Emma. And she was perfect for me; Emma made me feel needed again since I was not able to work at the hospital or fire department anymore. That made me happy! Having Emma showed me that I could still do something really important- I could rescue horses!

One night while in the barn, I looked into Emma's eyes and said, "I love you, Emma. You don't have to worry; this is going to be your last stop!" It was then that "Last Stop Horse Rescue" began and throughout the years many others have come to my farm to be loved just like Emma!

BELLE'S STORY: The Gentle Giant

Horses are what we call "herd" animals. A *herd* is a group of animals that enjoy being together. It makes them feel safe and because of that, I wanted Emma to have a friend.

I found Belle; a big Clydesdale horse. My heart told me to help her. Belle was sick with a very bad cough. She also needed food and water. Her face looked sad and I could tell she was lonely so I took her home to be Emma's friend.

When Belle arrived at my farm, something unexpected happened. Belle became angry and afraid. She was also very mean to me. Every time I came near her, she would try to kick me! This was so strange! What could have had happened to make Belle so dangerous? Whatever it was, I know it was not her fault because animals are not born mean.

A baby horse is called a *foal*. When Belle was a foal, she was an innocent little baby. She was not born angry or dangerous; something- or *someone* not very nice- probably made her that way. So instead of just getting rid of her, I decided to do my best to help her. I would not force Belle to do anything. And I would never punish her; I would only love her.

Each day, I would sit in the barn holding a bowl of grain on my lap while Belle ate from it. I would do the same with bales of hay out in the field. Over time, Belle figured out that I was someone she could trust. Within 3 months, I was riding her bareback!

Belle and I have taught each other many new things. She taught me how horses, especially unhappy horses, like to be approached by humans. They want to be treated kindly. And they look for leadership, but it must be loving leadership. If I want Belle to do something, I ask her nicely. By asking in a kind manner, Belle enjoys doing things for me. I never use force because you cannot make a horse do something; you can only ask them. And when I ask Belle, she says, "Yes, I will do that for you, because I love you and I trust you."

Today, Belle is the biggest and strongest horse at the farm. She is also one of the gentlest horses. But as big as Belle appears, she is still easily frightened by little things. Because of this, she will stay with me forever. Belle's story was Last Stop Horse Rescue's first miracle.

GRACIE'S STORY: Friends forever

Gracie is as small as Belle is big! Remember how herd animals they like to stick together? Well Gracie is part of a very special herd of miniature horses that came to the rescue after their owner passed away. It was very important that the herd remained together because Gracie was going to have a baby!

Soon after they arrived, Gracie's foal was born. We named her Lily and she was white just like her mommy!

As Lily grew older, she became adventurous and wanted to play with her friends. Her mommy did not like this very much; it was hard letting her baby go- even if it was just to the other side of the pasture!

But then we found out something else was causing Gracie to feel nervous. Remember learning about how animals are able to talk to us? That the way an animal moves can show us how they feel? Well we began noticing that Gracie was walking funny. Whenever she walked, she always needed something to lean against for security. I called the veterinarian to come look at Gracie.

After his exam, the veterinarian told me that Gracie had become blind. That meant Gracie could not see anymore! If she could not see, that was probably why she needed to *feel* Lily in order to know she was safe. But how was I going to explain that to a miniature horse? How was I going to tell Lily that her mommy was blind and needed another horse to help guide her?

To my amazement, a miracle happened! Big Belle, my "gentle giant", sensed little Gracie needed help. The unlikely pair suddenly became best friends- a small white miniature horse and a big brown Clydesdale!

They are always together. Belle even shares her food with Gracie! Learning to share is very important because it teaches us to care about other people. Because Belle cares so much about Gracie not being able to see, Gracie is able to live like any other horse on the farm, only her sight is guided by the love of big Belle.

The lesson I learned from Gracie and Belle is that the greatest of friendships can come in all shapes and sizes no matter how different they may be.

ANGEL'S STORY: A mother's love

Patsy's Angel is a beautiful black horse that was in need of my help. She was living in a place where nobody took care of her.

Angel was kept tied up in a small pen with no food or water, and no one to love her. When I first met Angel, although she was scared, she was still very kind. She did not try to hurt me the way Belle first did. Angel was just afraid of having a halter put on her.

A *halter* is a soft rope that gently goes over a horse's head so that a person can walk it on a leash just like a big dog! Most horses enjoy being walked by someone they love and trust but for Angel, just the sight of a halter was enough to make her want to run away! She was terrified! So I brought Angel to Last Stop Horse Rescue where she could see other horses and how I took care of them- some even wore halters!

Soon Angel learned what halters were used for. She also saw many horses wearing halters that had the freedom to run and play with other horses. This made her happy!

Something else was about to make Angel happy...

A local sheep farmer called to tell us one of his sheep had just given birth to twin lambs. This was exciting news! But the farmer sounded sad on the phone. He explained that the mommy sheep could not take care of two lambs. This meant that one of the twins needed a new mother!

Even though I rescue mostly horses, this baby lamb needed my help! So I picked her up from the sheep farm, carried her home in my arms and named her Annabelle.

Having Annabelle was just like having a real baby! She drank milk from a bottle, wore a diaper, and even slept in the house with me!

The horses were curious about this new funny looking friend that went "Baaaaaa" instead of "Neigh!" So I carried Annabelle around the farm and introduced her to each horse.

Of all the horses at the rescue, *Angel* looked at Annabelle and decided she wanted to be her new mommy! Angel rested her head on Annabelle's face and kissed her on her nose. She knew this innocent little lamb needed love and protection. It did not matter whether it was a baby horse or sheep; a mother's love is unconditional.

LIBBY'S STORY: A new family

Like horses, there are many other animals that need loving homes! If you are thinking about getting a pet, a great place to find one is at your local animal shelter. There are lots of dogs and cats waiting for a family to bring them home and love them forever.

One day I met a very special person who wanted to help animals. Her name is Noreen. She and I became good friends. Noreen was sad because her friend, Lori, had recently passed away. Lori had two dogs, Libby and Boogie. Libby is a dog with special needs. She is blind and cannot see because she was born with no eyes! With Lori now in Heaven, who was going to take care of her dogs? Who was going to help Libby?

I told Noreen not to worry because I would help no matter what it took! And it was going to take a lot because Libby and Boogie lived very far away. With the help of many friends, Libby and Boogie were able to fly to my farm on a big airplane so they could come live with me and the other animals at Last Stop Horse Rescue. It was a new beginning!

Libby had to learn her way around, but she adjusted quickly because even though she could not see, she could feel how much I loved her.

And then, a miracle happened! When I introduced Libby to Annabelle the lamb, Libby came over and started licking her like a mother dog would care for her puppies. I think Annabelle enjoyed it too because she just played along pretending to be a puppy! And I do not think Libby even figured it out! But Libby *was* about to figure something else out... her new "family" was about to get bigger!

My friend's pet goat had just given birth to five baby goats. One of the baby goats was born sick, weak and smaller than its siblings. The veterinarian said this little goat was going to need a lot of special care in order to survive. I wondered, "Maybe Libby would want to be this goat's mommy too?" So I decided to bring her home to the farm.

I was right! Libby immediately helped care for the baby goat as if her own! We named her Sophie. Sophie and Annabelle's friendship is so special because they now share Libby as a mommy.

Friendship in itself is a miracle. My friend Noreen, with her 5 grandchildren, Kristina, Anthony, Max, Anna & Aidan, will now be able to visit Libby at the rescue anytime they would like. And I believe that when they *see* Libby, they will *feel* Lori's spirit.

The lesson I learned from Libby, Annabelle, and Sophie is that sad stories can have happy endings. We can meet new friends in ways we did not know were possible. You do not need eyes to feel love. And love is what makes a family. Libby was given a beautiful blessing when she found hers!

CHIPPER'S STORY: Love knows no distance

Do you like Baseball? My grandson, Kenny, loves baseball and is a great player! Kenny also has a horse, Chipper-on-Third, named after a famous baseball player. Well Chipper does not actually belong to Kenny, he belongs to Farmer Bill. But Kenny loves Chipper as if he were his own horse because Chipper is extra special.

Remember Emma's story? She was my first pony- the one that nobody wanted because she could not be ridden. Well Chipper is a horse that anybody can ride! And he is perfect for children because he knows just what to do! This is because Chipper was trained by Farmer Bill who grew up on a farm with many different animals.

Do you know what makes my grandson a great baseball player? He works hard practicing his skills! Kenny also loves to ride horses. But for Kenny to ride horses as well as he plays baseball, he would need to practice that too!

Chipper is the perfect horse for Kenny to practice on because he is safe and enjoys being ridden! Over the summer, Kenny spent time visiting Chipper with

"Farmer Bill with Kenny and Kimberly on Chipper"
by Deb Lindsay

his mommy. They learned many new things together. Chipper helped them to be comfortable around horses. Some people are nervous around horses because they are so big and powerful, but Chipper makes my daughter and grandchildren feel safe. They know he would never hurt them because he loves them! And because of Chipper, my grandchildren are not afraid of the horses at my farm. I am very thankful for that!

Even though Chipper does not live at Last Stop Horse Rescue, I visit him often because he is so special! My granddaughter, Kimberly, comes with me wearing her "Chipper boots" and cowgirl hat. And we always come with carrots!

When we arrive, Chipper recognizes our voices and comes over to greet us with kisses!

The lesson I learned from Chipper is that you can love a horse even if they do not belong to you. It does not matter where the horse lives because "love knows no distance." When a horse gives you its heart, you will have it forever. And horses have very big hearts! Chipper's heart is big enough for Farmer Bill, his family, *and* my grandchildren! There may even be a horse at my farm waiting to give their heart to you! And remember... it is OK if you do not live near your horse because you will know in your hearts that you love each other no matter where you are- near or far!

If there is a horse at my farm that is special to you, I would love for you to maybe write them a letter or send them a picture. You could also help by sending a bag a grain or a bale of hay for them to eat!

LUCKY'S STORY: The kindness of strangers

I have had many horses come to me in need of food and water. Horses need a lot to eat because they are so big.

There was a horse named Lucky. Her name was "Lucky" but she was not very *lucky* at all.

Poor Lucky was not able to eat. She tried her best but could not swallow her food. This was because it hurt her to chew it. I did everything I could to help her. I put water in her grain to make it soft like soup and I even took her to see a horse dentist!

Months passed by and Lucky was not getting any better. I searched and searched until finally a miracle happened! I found a horse doctor at a special animal hospital who wanted to help Lucky! The hospital was very far away but that did not matter. I promised Lucky that I would never give up!

I loaded Lucky into a horse trailer and drove her 8 hours to the hospital. When we got there the doctors found a lump in Lucky's jaw. They said the lump was going to get bigger and needed to be removed. That meant Lucky needed to have an operation! And if she did not have this surgery, she could die! We were very sad. But this surgery was going to cost a lot of money.

I brought Lucky home. For two years I worked hard to help Lucky feel better while trying to raise money to pay for her surgery.

All of a sudden, Lucky became "*LUCKY!*" When people heard how expensive it was going to cost to save her life, everyone wanted to help!

Next, a very special veterinarian named Doctor Jennifer Rawlinson called and said, "I know I am very far away; but if you can bring Lucky to me, I will do the surgery!"

I could not believe it! Two years had gone by and there we were again- loading Lucky into my trailer for another road trip! Only this time she was going to come home all better... and she did! Doctor Rawlinson saved Lucky's life! She was our miracle!

The lesson I learned from Lucky's story is that anything is possible as long as you believe in miracles and never give up hope. Miracles do happen! God answers our prayers; He sends people into our lives when we need them most. And it is just as important for us to be a "miracle" to someone else.

"Doctor Jennifer Rawlinson and Joyce celebrating Lucky's life" by Deb Lindsay

You can help rescue animals too!

I hope you enjoyed reading my stories and learning about Last Stop Horse Rescue! Maybe someday you can come visit my farm and meet the animals in this book. I would love to share more about how you can help horses. If you cannot visit us, there are lots of things you can still do to make a difference for animals where you live:

1. Always be kind and gentle to animals. Try to stay calm around them. Talk softly and never do anything that could frighten them.

2. If you see someone being mean to an animal, find a grown-up and tell them immediately.

3. If you find an animal that is injured, do not touch it. Sometimes when an animal is hurt, they become scared and could hurt the person trying to help them. Find a grown-up so they can call for help.

4. Tell your parents that you would like to volunteer at a local animal shelter. There are many animal shelters that help dogs, cats, and other pets find new homes with families who will love them forever. Animal Shelters need people like you to walk dogs, clean cages, and feed the animals. Being there will also help teach the animals to trust people. They will learn that you are there to love and care for them, not hurt them. This will help them to feel safe in their new homes.

5. If you belong to a group like Girl Scouts, Boy Scouts, 4-H, or something similar, you can help your local rescue by doing fundraisers to help feed the animals. These fundraisers can include bake sales, collecting food donations, or you could even help sell this book! All the money earned from this book is being used to help feed the animals you just read about!

6. Remember these lessons from the animals at Last Stop Horse Rescue and think about ways you can help others to also '*Believe in Miracles.*'

To learn more about Last Stop Horse Rescue, please visit us at:

http://www.laststophorserescue.com/

A Message from the Writer

I helped write this book because I wholeheartedly believe in its purpose. Not only does it teach children beautiful lessons of love and friendship, it is also going to help many horses in need by having its proceeds benefit Last Stop Horse Rescue, a 501(c)3 non-profit organization.

In this book, you read stories about some of the animals Joyce has helped. But I wanted to share a different kind of story. Did you know that animals can help us also? Horses especially! God made horses with a special gift. He gave them the ability to sense when a human needs love. Horses can help people forget their troubles and feel happy!

To show you what I mean, I would like to share the following true story written by Jodi Carlton after she and her family recently visited Last Stop Horse Rescue:

"My son, Aidan, has always loved animals and has the softest, kindest heart. When he was 5 years old, he moved a worm off of the driveway so it wouldn't get crushed by the car. Because of his young age, our own dogs and cats never really give him much respect, treating him as more of a "pup" in their "pack." They just don't see him as having rank, I guess. Yet one day when we visited a horse rescue farm, Last Stop Horse Rescue, the horses there saw something entirely different when Aidan set foot in their pasture. According to Joyce Pomeroy, most of her horses have stories of abuse and neglect with emotional scars that have been much slower to heal than the physical wounds which have gradually disappeared with her tender love and care. Many of her horses are very distrustful of people and often shy away from visitors. Joyce always allows the horses to feel safe, and to interact with visitors based on their own comfort levels. One of her horses, Belle, is a large Clydesdale and usually keeps to herself. That day, however, Belle's ears perked up when she saw Aidan. She actually

Aidan and Spirit at Last Stop Horse Rescue, Pleasantville Meadow Farm, Gainesville, GA

left her area in the pasture where she had been eating and came over to greet Aidan! Joyce later told me that Belle responded to Aidan in a similar way to how she had responded to "Gracie", a miniature horse at the rescue who had gone blind and needed a friend to protect her. Belle followed Aidan around the pasture and at one point even put her ears back to move the other horses away from Aidan as if to say, "This is my little boy! Step away!" Belle knew what she was doing. She saw and sensed what the human eye could not. Belle recognized instantly that my son needed his own kind of rescuing. Not only did Belle see a boy who has a deep love for animals-someone she could instantly trust- she also saw a boy who had been deeply wounded himself. Aidan was diagnosed with Epilepsy when he was just 18 months old. His older sister has Asperger's, a high functioning form of Autism. Not many people can truly understand how tough that is for siblings. Aidan has also been bullied by children at school. This past Fall, Aidan became very ill with chronic infections, including a month long episode of low-grade fevers and having poor school attendance, all of which led to a relapse of his epilepsy. The day we visited Last Stop Horse Rescue, Joyce did not know any of this. We were essentially strangers. However, the horses greeted Aidan like a long-lost friend, and the feeling was mutual! They were drawn together like magnets. Belle eventually allowed the other horses to meet Aidan as well. He spent time brushing and loving each of them. Although he's never spent a lot of time with horses, particularly in a herd, Aidan was so comfortable and relaxed- he felt at peace. Although Belle appointed herself as Aidan's guardian, an undeniable bond with a second horse occurred. The horse's name – Spirit. And kindred spirits they are! Spirit was so at ease with Aidan that he laid down in the pasture beside him. Together they sat on the ground for the longest time, leaning their heads on each other, feeling loved and safe. I read a saying once: "Sometimes it takes a wounded healer to heal." I believe that my son needs these horses as much as they need him. The bond between them is more than I can describe. They seem to understand each other without needing any words at all. On Aidan's return visit to the farm he met one of the most damaged souls I have ever seen, a white Paso Fino horse named Murdock. He was full of fear and anger toward humans, but that only made Aidan love him more. Aidan was determined to show Murdock that he could trust humans and was loved. The way Murdock responded to Aidan was the type of miracle Joyce speaks of so often. I believe that animals and humans are so very closely connected- that we, as humans, have a responsibility to watch over the creatures of this Earth. Little did I realize how closely they are watching over us as well."

Thank you, Jodi, for sharing the beautiful experience your family had at my mother's farm and the lesson you learned from the horses at Last Stop Horse Rescue- "Sometimes it takes a wounded healer to heal." I dedicate my part in this book to your son, Aidan. May he never lose hope and always remember how special he is. God has blessed Aidan with a gift- a gift of healing. I was there during Aidan's visit to the farm and what I witnessed was something truly miraculous.

Always Believe in Miracles, Aidan; because I believe in you!

With Love and Blessings,
Toni Helen

Joyce Pomeroy, Founder of Last Stop Horse Rescue

Joyce has 3 daughters and 5 grandchildren. She is a retired Firefighter/EMT and worked 18 years managing a Cardiology practice. Joyce was also an EMT Instructor for New York State and taught various vocational medical classes as well. She recently expanded her rescue to a second location to be closer to her family. Last Stop Horse Rescue (LSHR) is a 501c3 non-profit organization, licensed in both Maine and Georgia, dedicated to saving abused, starved, and neglected horses. Each horse under their loving care is rehabilitated using Natural Horsemanship, no-force methods. LSHR works closely with Animal Welfare as well as state Veterinarian programs and relies on the generosity of friends and volunteers to help in their mission.

Toni Helen, Writer/Editor and Board Member

Toni's love for horses began during the most exciting 2 minutes in history! His name was Secretariat and he was known as the greatest racehorse to ever live! But *what happens to equine athletes after they cross their final finish line?* Toni helps Last Stop Horse Rescue to rescue and rehabilitate ex-race horses off the track and into her heart where she helps find them a new beginning. Toni enjoys cooking, treasure hunting, and spending quality time with her beloved Grandma Ginger. She is married with 2 children, Kenny and Kimberly. Together they share a buckskin horse named Pierogi, in memory of their Grandpa "Soulmate".

Deb Lindsay, Illustrator and Board Member

Growing up, Deb loved horses. She especially loved to draw them! Deb's dad put her on a horse before she was old enough to even walk! Deb wanted to provide a safe place for unwanted horses- it was her dream. In 1995, Deb's dream came true. She started Forever Home Equine Sanctuary where she now lives with 8 horses, 6 cats, and a dog. Over the years, Deb's passion for art and drawing horses continued. When sketching an animal, Deb strives to capture the emotion of that animal as well as the person seeing it. She hopes her hand-drawn pictures in this book will touch the hearts of many children and bring these stories to life for them. To see more of Deb Lindsay's beautiful artwork, please visit: http://www.deblindsayequineart.com/

$15.00 U.S. / $16.00 Canada

ISBN 978-0-69-261051-0

PROCEEDS TO BENEFIT LAST STOP HORSE RESCUE

© Copyright 2015
All rights reserved.

www.ingramcontent.com/pod-product-compliance
Lightning Source LLC
Chambersburg PA
CBHW060808090426
42736CB00002B/196